DAY HIKES ON
O A H U

by Robert Stone

Photographs by Robert Stone
Published by:
Day Hike Books, Inc.
114 South Hauser Box 865
Red Lodge, Mt. 59068
Copyright 1994

Distributed by:
ICS Books, Inc.
1370 E. 86th Place
Merrillville, In. 46410
1-800-541-7323
Fax 1-800-336-8334

ABOUT THE HIKES

When most people think of Oahu, they imagine the city of Honolulu along with the beaches and skyline of Waikiki. Oahu has so much more to offer. The hikes and locations in this book allow any visitor or family additional areas to enjoy as well as examples of how much diversity this Hawaiian Island has.

This hiking guide concentrates on scenic day hikes of various lengths. My goal is to share these hikes with others in an easy-to-understand manner. This method enables visitors and locals to enjoy the backcountry more easily.

All the hikes in this book require easy to moderate effort. The elevation gains are listed. They are all timed at a leisurely rate. As I hike, I enjoy looking at trees, clouds, flowers, spiders and streams; I like to savor the pleasures of nature. The time given for each hike allows for daydreams and study. If you wish to hike faster or go further, the hikes are equally rewarding.

As for attire and equipment, tennis shoes, as opposed to hiking boots are fine for any of these hikes. A rain poncho, sunscreen and mosquito repellent are recommended. Drinking water is a must. The trails can be (and usually are) slippery due to rain and mud, so use caution. Pack a lunch for a picnic at pools, streams, scenic overlooks or wherever you find the best spot.

With this in mind, enjoy the hikes!

TABLE OF CONTENTS

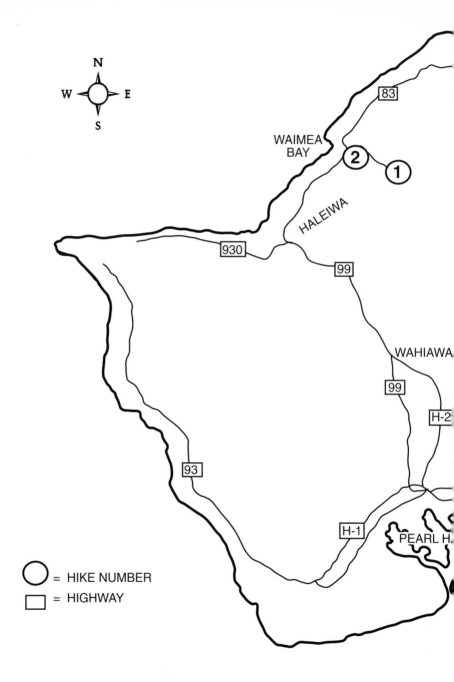

= HIKE NUMBER

= HIGHWAY

MAP OF THE HIKES

KAHUKU

LAIE

HAUULA

③

④

KAHANA

⑤

⑥

⑦

83

836

Kahekili Hwy.

LIKELIKE HWY.

78

PALI HWY.

63

⑨

H-1

61

⑩

⑫

⑪

⑬

H-1

RT

⑮

WAIKIKI

⑭ DIAMOND HEAD

Hike 1
KAUNALA LOOP

Open to the public on weekends and holidays only.
Do not let the "Private Property-No Trespassing" signs stop you.
Staying on the road to the foot trail is permissible.

5 mile hike round trip
3 hours
1000' elevation gain

Summary of hike: This hike is exceptional. It has everything from dense, lush, tropical forests to open, panoramic views; from a stream crossing in a gulch to ridge views from the Waianae Mountains to the ocean. An abundance of paperback eucalyptus, ohia, kukui, ironwood, mahogany, silk, oak, and Norfolk pine trees surround this hike.

Driving directions: Take H-1 west to H-2. Take H-2 north to Wahiawa, where H-2 ends. Continue north on Route 99 to Haleiwa. Drive east through Haleiwa, and stay on this north shore road (83) past Waimea Falls Park on the right. Turn right on Pupukea Road. (A supermarket is on this corner.) Pupukea Road climbs sharply. Continue on this road until it ends at the gate. This is the gate with private property notices. Park off the road near the gate.
The drive is approximately 41 miles from Waikiki.

Hiking directions: Hike to the end of the public road to a locked military gate. Go around the gate, and sign in at Hunters' "sign-in" booth. Hike along the road for about a half mile, and watch for a foot trail on the left. The trail begins here and so does the magnificence of this hike.
　　Stay on the main foot trail. This trail will descend to the stream bed. After crossing the stream, the trail climbs slowly until the foot trail meets the vehicle trail again. Turn right and hike upward along the ridge. Go around the "Government - No Trespassing" gate. Turn right on the main trail. This trail will loop back to the car.

Hike 2
PUU O MAHUKA STATE MONUMENT

A short side hike on the way to the
Kaunala Loop (Hike 1)

1/4 to 1/2 mile round trip
30 minutes
Level hiking

Summary of hike: This hike wanders around one of Oahu's oldest temples. Once used for human sacrifice, this *Heiau* (religious temple of ancient Hawaiian culture) overlooks Waimea Bay. (See back cover photo.) Rocks outline the site. The *Heiau* always has fresh offerings of ti leaves wrapped around rocks, leis and fruit. These are religious offerings, so please be respectful.

Driving directions: Take H-1 west to H-2. Take H-2 north to Wahiawa, where H-2 ends. Continue north on Route 99 to Haleiwa. Drive east through Haleiwa, and stay on this north shore road (83) past Waimea Falls Park on the right. Turn right on Pupukea Road. (A supermarket is on this corner.) Pupukea Road climbs sharply. Turn right on Puu o Mahuka Road. This narrow road ends at a parking lot at the Heiau State Monument.
The drive is approximately 40 miles from Waikiki.

Hiking directions: Hike around the *Heiau*. Well-defined paths encircle the site.

Hike 3
HAUULA LOOP TRAIL

3 mile hike round trip
2 hours
750' elevation gain

Summary of hike: This hike offers great views of the valley, the mountains, the ocean, and the town of Hauula. There is a large variety of trees. Among them are Norfolk pine, paperback eucalyptus, ironwood, African tulip, octopus, and guava trees.

Driving directions: Take H-1 west to H-2. Take H-2 north to Wahiawa, where H-2 ends. Continue north on Route 99 to Haleiwa. Drive east through Haleiwa and stay on the north shore road (83). Drive past the north point and continue past the towns of Kahuku and Laie. 2.5 miles past the Polynesian Cultural Center, turn right on Kukuna Road. This turn is between highway mile markers 21 and 22 by the town of Hauula. Drive on Kukuna Road to the stop sign and turn right. Drive 0.2 miles to Maakua Road and turn left. Go one block and park at the end of the road.
The drive is approximately 55 miles from Waikiki.

Hiking directions: After parking, walk inland to the trail sign. After crossing the dry creek bed, watch for the trail that branches off sharply to the right. (The left trail is the beginning of the Maakua Ridge Loop - Hike 4). For this hike , go to the right. The trail gently climbs with the aid of several switchbacks. Shortly thereafter is the beginning of the loop. To hike clockwise, take the left fork. Stay on the main trail as it winds around along the ridge overlooking the canyons, mountains, and ocean. The trail will decend into Waipilopilo Gulch and cross a stream. Upon completing the loop, turn left and return to your car.

Hike 4
PAPALI / MAAKUA RIDGE LOOP

3 mile hike round trip
2 hours
750' elevation gain

Summary of hike: This hike is a beautiful forest and ridge hike overlooking the town of Hauula, the ocean and the mountains,

Driving directions: Take H-1 west to H-2. Take H-2 north to Wahiawa, where H-2 ends. Continue north on Route 99 to Haleiwa. Drive east through Haleiwa and stay on the north shore road (83). Drive past the north point and continue past the towns of Kahuku and Laie. 2.5 miles past the Polynesian Cultural Center, turn right on Kukuna Road. This turn is between highway mile markers 21 and 22 by the town of Hauula. Drive on Kukuna Road to the stop sign and turn right. Drive 0.2 miles to Maakua Road and turn left. Go one block and park at the end of the road.
The drive is approximately 55 miles from Waikiki.

Hiking directions: Walk inland to the trail sign. After crossing the dry creek bed, stay on the road. Pass the trail on the right which leads to the Hauula Trail (Hike 3). A little further on the main trail is a junction. Take the left trail up a switchback to beautiful views. The loop portion of the hike begins here. To hike this loop counterclockwise, take the right trail. Hike from the ridge to the gulch, crossing a stream and zigzagging up to the ridge again to complete the loop. Bear right, taking this trail back to the main road and to your car.

Hike 5
SACRED FALLS

4 mile hike round trip
2.5 hours
500' elevation gain

Summary of hike: This hike is a beautiful forested trail with stream crossings. The trail ends at the waterfall and swimming pool. (See cover photo.)

Driving directions: Take H-1 west to Likelike Highway (63), heading northeast to the Windward Coast. After crossing the mountains, there are two driving options. You may take the shorter, more direct route - the Kahekili Highway (83) - turning left (north) off the Likelike Highway. Your second option is to take the more scenic, but longer route - the Kamehameha Highway (836). The junction for the 836 is about a 1/2 mile further on the Likelike Highway (63). Both the 83 and the 836 merge together when Highway 83 meets the coast. Approximately 3.5 miles past the well-marked Kahana Valley State Park is the not-so-well-marked parking lot for Sacred Falls. The lot sits behind a hedge. It is 200' south of the Old Hawaiian Church, a noticeable old church house. If you spot the church, you have passed the parking lot. The drive is about 30 miles from Waikiki.

Hiking directions: The trail begins across from the parking lot by the "Flash Flooding" sign. From the trailhead, walk along a cane road for about 1.3 miles to the end. Several benches, trees, and a grassy park area offer a resting or picnic spot. The trail then becomes a narrow footpath through dense forest following the Kaluanui Stream. Further along, past several large boulders, is the first stream crossing. After crossing the stream, the canyon begins to narrow. With 1500-foot canyon walls, the Kaluanui Stream cascading down, and the lush vegetation, it is easy to understand why this land is "sacred." Cross the stream again, and you are at the base of a large pool and a 90-foot waterfall. Hike back to your car on the same trail.

View of ocean from Kahana State Park - Hike 6.

A view from Maakua Ridge - Hike 4.

Hike 6
KAHANA VALLEY STATE PARK
KAPAELEELE LOOP
(1st of 2 hikes)

1.2 mile hike round trip
45 minutes
150' elevation gain

Summary of hike: This hike includes beautiful views of Kahana Bay and two cultural shrines. The trails are maintained by the Boy Scouts. The Park Headquarters, located by the parking lot, has historical pamphlets with trail maps.

Driving directions: Take H-1 west to Likelike Highway (63) heading northeast to the Windward Coast. After crossing the mountains, there are two driving options. You may take the shorter, more direct route - The Kahekili Highway (83) - turning left (north) off the Likelike Highway. Your second option is to take the more scenic, but longer route - the Kamehameha Highway (836). The junction for the 836 is about a 1/2 mile further on the Likelike Highway (63). Both the 83 and the 836 merge together when Highway 83 meets the coast. As you near Kahana Valley State Park, the road curves left at Mahie Point, where you will be overlooking Kahana Bay. Watch on the left for the Kahana Valley State Park sign. Turn left into the parking area. The drive is approximately 26 miles from Waikiki.

Hiking directions: From the parking area, walk past the Park Headquarters building to the trailhead. The trail is marked. There are two, old Hawaiian religious shrines on this hike where fishermen pray for good fishing. There is a short, uphill trail to "Keaniani Kilo" for the best view of Kahana Bay. Then, return to the main trail. The trail switchbacks to the highway. Cross the highway and return to your car via the beach.

Hike 7
KAHANA VALLEY STATE PARK
NAKOA TRAIL to Swimming Hole
(2nd of 2 hikes)

3 mile hike round trip
2 hours
300' elevation gain

Summary of hike: This hike includes several stream crossings en route to a mountain stream swimming pool by a dam.

Driving directions: Take H-1 west to Likelike Highway (63), heading northeast to the Windward Coast. After crossing the mountains, there are two driving options. You may take the shorter, more direct route - the Kahekili Highway (83) - turning left (north) off the Likelike Highway. Your second option is to take the more scenic, but longer route - the Kamehameha Highway (836). The junction for the 836 is about a 1/2 mile further on the Likelike Highway (63). Both the 83 and the 836 merge together when Highway 83 meets the coast. As you near Kahana Valley State Park, the road curves left at Mahie Point, where you will be overlooking Kahana Bay. Watch on the left for the Kahana Valley State Park sign. Turn left into the parking area. The drive is approximately 26 miles from Waikiki.

Hiking directions: Follow the main road up the Kahana Valley past residential homes to the gate. Pass the gate and take the right fork when the road splits. The road will divide a second time in about one mile. Take the left fork onto the narrower trail. This is the beginning of the Nakoa Trail. As you approach and cross Kahana Stream, you will see the dam and a large swimming pool. This is our destination spot. After swimming, retrace your steps.

A green fern pool near Jackass Ginger Trail - Hike 9.

Rainbow over Ala Wai Canal - Hike 15.

A view of Waikiki from Diamond Head - Hike 14.

The author dwarfed by ancient tree - Foster Botanical Gardens - Hike 11.

Hike 8
KEAIWA HEIAU STATE PARK
AIEA LOOP

5 mile hike round trip
3 hours
1000' elevation gain

Summary of hike: Trails located in the popular Keaiwa Heiau State Park are well-used and well-maintained. There are beautiful picnic areas with pavilions. The hiking trails wind through eucalyptus and Norfolk pine forests.

Driving directions: Take H-1 west to Highway 78 to Aiea. (Stay in the left lanes for the Highway 78 junction.) Take the Aiea exit onto Moanalua Road. From Moanalua Road, turn right on Aiea Heights Drive. Aiea Heights Drive winds its way into Keaiwa Heiau State Park. Drive on this one way road to its highest point, and park in the parking lot by the trailhead.
Keaiwa Heiau State Park is approximately 14 miles from Waikiki.

Hiking directions: The trailhead is at the back of the parking lot by the water tank. The trail begins at a eucalyptus forest with a magnificent tree route system woven across the path. Shortly after is a level viewing area of Honolulu. The main trail follows along the ridge. The ridge has alternating views of the city on the right and the seemingly endless mountains on the left. As you pass the far end of the loop and begin heading back, watch the gully for wreckage of a C47 cargo plane from a 1943 crash. Shortly after, the trail descends to the Aiea Stream. Near the end of the hike, climb the steps to the right of a camping area to the main road. Turn right again, going uphill to your car.

Hike 9
JUDD MEMORIAL TRAIL
JACKASS GINGER POOL

1 mile hike round trip
Half hour plus play time
200' elevation gain

Summary of hike: This trail is a loop, but most people, (myself included) prefer to go straight to the cascading waters and swimming pools.

Driving directions: Take H-1 to the Pali Highway (61) north. Drive two miles on the Pali Highway to Nuuanu Pali Drive. Take the turnoff to the right and stay on Nuuanu Pali Drive for one mile. Take the right fork at the junction, continuing on Nuuanu Pali Drive. The parking lot is on the right, shortly after Poli Hiwa Place. A small sign marks the parking lot.
The drive is approximately six miles from Waikiki.

Hiking directions: From the parking lot, walk down to the stream and cross over it with the help of large rocks. If you miss a rock and get wet, it is okay; you are here to swim anyway! Take the trail uphill through bamboo, Norfolk pines, and hau trees. Watch and listen to your right for the stream and pools. The trail will quickly descend to the pool. To return, either retrace your steps along the main trail or, as I prefer, walk upstream to the original stream crossing. You should recognize the crossing and will see the parking area. Along the way, you will pass more swimming holes.

Manoa Falls and swimming pool - Hike 10.

Hike 10
MANOA FALLS

2 mile hike round trip
1 hour
400, elevation gain

Summary of Hike: This hike expolores a beautiful rain forest of dense vegetation with a wonderful waterfall and swimming pool.

Driving directions: From Waikiki, take McCully (the first bridge crossing over Ala Wai Canal) past H-1 to Wilder Avenue. Turn left and drive to Punahou Street (less than 1/2 mile). Turn right on Punahou Street which shortly becomes Manoa Road. Take the left fork when the road divides, staying on Manoa Road. Further up, at a 4-way crossing, bear right, again staying on Manoa Road. Drive past the Paradise Park parking lot. The Manoa Falls Trail is about 1 block past this parking lot. Park on the short trailhead road before the main road curves sharply to the left towards the Lyon Arboretum (Hike 13).
The drive is approximately four miles from Waikiki.

Hiking directions: From the trailhead, hike slightly uphill, crossing a bridge over Aihualama Stream. Veer left and stay on this muddy main trail following along Waihi Stream. A network of beautifully tangled tree roots create a web pattern on the trail. As you near Manoa Falls, the valley narrows and the trail climbs. At the base of Manoa Falls is a shallow, yet large, pool. Return on the same route.

Hike 11
FOSTER BOTANICAL GARDENS

1/2 to 1 mile hike round trip
1 to 2 hours
level hiking

Summary of hike: Foster Botanical Gardens is on the National Register of Historic Places, and what a place! This 140-year-old living museum sits on 13.5 acres. It has a cross section of plant life ranging from orchid gardens to spice gardens, from palms and gingers to coffee and chocolate trees. Some of the plants are rare, some are endangered, some are native to Hawaii, some come from countries all over the world. There is a small entrance fee.

Driving directions: From Waikiki, take McCully (the first bridge crossing over Ala Wai Canal) to Beretania Street. (Beretania Street comes before H-1.) Turn left and drive 2.4 miles to Nuuanu. Turn right on Nuuanu, and stay on this road to the next major intersection, which is Vineyard Boulevard. Foster Botanical Gardens is on the northwest corner of this intersection. Turn left on Vineyard to the parking lot. Foster Gardens is three miles from Waikiki.

Hiking directions: You may wander around the pathways and stretches of lawn. Everyone is drawn to different things in different directions. You cannot get lost. A helpful map is available at the entrance.

Hike 12
KANEALOLE TRAIL
(Hawaii Nature Center)

1 1/2 mile hike round trip
1 hour
500' elevation gain

Summary of hike: This area has an abundance of excellent hikes with well-maintained trails. They are all centered near the Hawaii Nature Center. The Nature Center is devoted to helping preserve Hawaii's environment. This center had educational displays on plant and animal life in Hawaii. It also has regularly planned hikes on weekends. You may contact the Nature Center at (808) 955-0100.

The Kanealole Trail is one of eleven hiking trails in the area. They are all exceptional hikes, from a half mile to eight miles in length. They range from valley hikes with intimate surroundings, to ridge hikes with superb views.

Maps are available at the Nature Center.

Driving directions: From Waikiki, take McCully (the first bridge crossing of Ala Wai Canal) to Wilder Avenue. Turn left on Wilder and go about 1/2 mile to Makiki Street. Turn right on Makiki. A half mile up the road, take the left fork at a triangular park. This road is Makiki Heights Drive which sharply curves to the left. Do not take the switchback. Instead, go straight (north) onto the smaller road, which leads into Makiki Valley. Park on the side of the road at the park just below the Hawaii Nature Center.
The Nature Center is two miles from Waikiki.

Hiking directions: Walk to the end of the main road. It quickly becomes a footpath. This hike is slightly uphill all the way. This happily means it is slightly downhill all the way back.

Hike 13
LYON ARBORETUM
Open 9 a.m. to 3 p.m. Mon.- Sat.

Hike 1: 1 mile round trip
Hike 2: 1/2 mile round trip
Small elevation gain

Summary of hike: Lyon Arboretum is an active research facility and public tropical garden on 194 acres in the Manoa Valley. As a part of the University of Hawaii, this facility is instrumental in conservation biology, horticulture, and ethnobotany research.

Driving directions: From Waikiki, take McCully (the first bridge crossing over Ala Wai Canal) past H-1 to Wilder Avenue. Turn left and drive to Punahou Street (less than 1/2 mile). Turn right on Punahou Street, which shortly becomes Manoa Road. Take the left fork when the road divides, staying on Manoa Road. Further up, at a 4-way crossing, bear right, again staying on Manoa Road. Drive past the Paradise Park parking lot. The Arboretum is a 1/2 mile further. The road will take a sharp bend to the left. The Arboretum is at the end of this road. The drive is four miles from Waikiki.

Hiking directions: There are two hiking trails here. A one-mile walking road passes the Hawaiian Ethnobotanical Garden; the research area; the exotic palm, banyon, macadamia, and ginger trees; and a great deal more. The second hike is approximately 1/2 mile of meandering through garden paths and grass up to Inspiration Point. A walking guide through the gardens is available at the registration office and gift shop.

Hike 14
DIAMOND HEAD

1-1/2 mile hike round trip
1-1/4 hours
550' elevation gain

Summary of hike: This trail leads you inside a 760-foot volcano that has been dormant for 150,000 years (give or take 30 years). After climbing out of the crater, the hike offers a variety of lookouts along the trail, including panoramic views of Waikiki, the ocean and Koko Head. Known to Hawaiians as "Leahi," Diamond Head is considered a "symbol of Hawaii."

Driving directions: From Waikiki, drive southeast on Kalakaua Avenue the main street running through Waikiki. Curve to the left (east) onto Monsarrat Avenue. Monsarrat Avenue becomes Diamond Head Road. Turn right into Diamond Head State Monument. This road leads through a tunnel and to the parking area.
The drive is approximately two miles from Waikiki.

Hiking directions: A paved walkway from the parking area leads to the trail. The trail climbs along the interior of the crater. About halfway up, stairs lead to a dark tunnel. Although a handrail will lead you through, a flashlight is recommended. After the tunnel, 99 stairs lead up a spiral staircase to a bunker at the top. As you climb out of the bunker, you are overlooking the ocean, Waikiki, Honolulu, and the Koko Head crater. The view is tremendous.

Hike 15
ALA WAI CANAL

0.5 to 3.5 mile round trip
10 minutes to 2 hours
Level hiking

Summary of hike: A calm and beautiful stroll, the Ala Wai Canal is a paved walkway from the marina through the length of Waikiki. The canal runs parallel to the ocean only a few blocks inland. Regardless of where you start, this hike has pretty scenery, other walkers, joggers, kayakers, canoists, and hoards of fish wishing to be fed.

Driving directions: Don't drive . . . walk! If you are staying in Waikiki, it is only a couple of blocks from the ocean. Walk inland three blocks and you are there.

Hiking directions: You may start and finish anywhere along the walkway.

NOTES

BIBLIOGRAPHY

Ball, Stuart M. *The Hikers Guide To Oahu.*
Univ. of Hawaii Press, 1993.

Bisignani, J.D. *Hawaii Handbook.*
Chico, CA: Moon Pub., 1989.

Chisholm, Craig. *Hawaiian Hiking Trails.*
7th ed. Lake Oswego, OR: Fernglen Press, 1991.

Morey, Kathy. *Oahu Trails.* Berkeley, CA:
Wilderness Press, 1993.

Riegert, Ray. *Hidden Hawaii.* 7th ed.
Berkeley, CA: Ulysses Press, 1993.

Smith, Rodney N. *Hawaii: A Walker's Guide.*
Edison, NJ: Hunter Pub., no year listed.

Sullivan, Richard. *Driving and Discovering Oahu.*
Los Angeles: Montgomery Ewing Pub., 1993.

TOM EGENES

ABOUT THE AUTHOR

An avid hiker for many years, Robert Stone has found the Hawaiian Islands a hiking paradise. He has hiked and photographed extensively throughout Asia, Europe, the Caribbean, Hawaiian Islands and the United States. When not traveling, Robert makes his home in the Rocky Mountains of Montana.

Other Day Hike Guidebooks

_____ Day Hikes on Maui . . . . $ 6.95

_____ Day Hikes on Kauai 6.95

_____ Day Hikes in Los Angeles
      Venice/Santa Monica to Topanga Canyon 6.95

_____ Day Hikes in Boulder, Colorado 6.95

_____ Day Hikes in Steamboat Springs, Colorado 6.95

_____ Day Hikes in Denver 6.95

_____ Day Hikes in Summit County, Colorado
      Breckenridge, Dillon, Frisco, Keystone, and Silverthorne 6.95

_____ Day Hikes in the Grand Tetons and Jackson Hole 6.95

_____ Day Hikes in Yellowstone National Park
      West Yellowstone to Old Faithful 6.95

_____ Day Hikes in Yellowstone National Park
      Ten Favorite Hikes 6.95

_____ Day Hikes in the Beartooths
      Red Lodge to Cooke City, Montana 4.95

These books may be purchased at your local bookstore or they will be glad to order them. For a full list of titles available from ICS Books, call toll-free 1-800-541-7323. Visa or Mastercard accepted. Please include $2.00 per order to cover postage and handling.

- -

Please send the books marked above. I enclose $_____

Name _____

Address _____

City _____ State _____ Zip _____

Credit Card # _____ Expires _____

Signature _____

Distributed by:
ICS Books, Inc.
1370 E. 86th Place, Merrillville, In. 46410
1-800-541-7323 • Fax 1-800-336-8334